The Summer of New Toys

Dedicated to my daughters Andrea and Cecelia.

Thank you for being my inspiration.

Copyright ©Anthony L. Surrette
All rights reserved.
ISBN-13: 978-0692573174
ISBN-10: 0692573178

The Summer of New Toys

by Anthony L. Surrette
Illustrated by Spuffs

The sun was shining, and it was the first official day of summer.

Alice and Pete were brother and sister.

They lived with their Mom and Dad in a beautiful brick home.

Alice was a sweet, energetic four-year-old. Pete was a charming, adventurous seven-year-old.

Alice had all of her favorite toys scattered over the floor in her large pink room.

Pete was across the hall in his bedroom, playing with his huge train set that took up most of the floor.

They had all the toys they wanted in the world. They were so happy!

It was Monday morning, and Alice's and Pete's parents were going away on a business trip.

They were going to be gone for most of the summer and decided to send the kids to stay with their grandparents.

Their grandparents had a beach house, and the kids were excited that they would be spending the summer there.

Alice dreamt of all the tea parties she would have with her dolls on the beach.

Pete thought of taking his superhero action figures with him, so they could have great adventures in the ocean.

The next morning, their bags were all packed, and you could see the excitement on everyone's faces.

While dragging her doll downstairs, Alice's mom said, "Darling, you will have to leave the doll behind as there is no room. The same goes for you Pete. There will be plenty of things for you to play with at your grandparents."

The children could not believe their ears. No toys?

How would their summer be fun without any of their favorite toys?

Alice was almost in tears, and Pete could not stop scowling.

They had the same thought going through their minds, "summer would be ruined."

On the way to their grandparents, Dad told stories of the summers he spent as a child on the beach.

It sounded like it would be a lot of fun and soon, their minds were off of the toys they left behind.

They began to wonder what new toys they would be able to play with.

They were starting to look forward to the trip to the beach.

When they arrived at the house, the children were excited.

They jumped out of the car as their bags were being taken inside the house.

Alice saw Grandpa first and ran into his embrace with her pigtails flying behind her.

Pete came soon after, and Grandpa ruffled his hair.

They said their goodbyes to their parents and went into the house.

When they were inside the house, the children looked around with curiosity and wonder.

They had never been to the beach house.

The only times they had seen their grandparents was when they came to visit at their home.

The house was huge on the inside, and a sweet smell came from the kitchen.

The children darted towards the smell and saw Grandma taking chocolate chip cookies out of the oven.

The table was set, and the children happily grabbed a seat, waiting for a cookie.

"Thank you so much, Grandma," the children chorused. "We are so happy to see you!"

The chocolate chip cookies were the best they had ever had. They had yummy, chewy chocolate in every bite.

After the delicious snack, the children were taken up to their room.

Grandpa told them bedtime stories until they both fell fast asleep. They were so exhausted.

The next morning, Alice woke up crying, as she could not find her bunny or the dolls that she usually slept with.

She had to be comforted by her grandma, who explained that the toys were still at her house.

Meanwhile, Pete was in high spirits, as he remembered all the fun their dad had promised they would have.

He could not wait to go exploring with his grandfather.

After breakfast, the children spent some time inside the house.

After a while, they got bored and wanted to know where the toys were.

"There are no toys in this house," said Grandpa.

Alice and Pete looked each other with disbelief.

"But Dad said he had lots of fun here as a kid. How did he do that if he did not have toys?" asked Pete.

"He had to buy his own toys, of course," Grandma said with a smile on her face.

Alice's face lit up immediately, "Oh, Grandma may we go buy some please? I'll have a tea party this evening, and all the princesses will be there."

"Of course we can, dear. Do you have any money?" Grandma asked.

Pete responded, "No, we don't."

Grandpa laughed and said, "Do you have any ideas on how you could get some money? Grandma and I will help you if you can think of anything."

Grandpa shared some of his ideas on how they could make money to buy toys.

The children did not have any of their own ideas, so they listened attentively, and wrote down a list.

They were glad that they would get to spend the money they earned on new toys.

Their excitement was so great the kids wanted to start immediately.

Grandma, however, wouldn't have it, as she thought that Alice and Pete should rest for the day.

They would begin the next day.

It was a bright morning, and the sun was shining over the beautiful beaches.

The children woke up and were reminded by Grandma that they would be starting work for their new toys.

Their first idea would be selling lemonade on the beach.

Alice helped Grandma make the lemonade, and Pete and Grandpa made a sign that read "Lemonade".

People started to line up and buy the lemonade for 25 cents a cup.

The children were so excited to be working with their grandparents.

At the end of the day, the children had sold many cups of lemonade at 25 cents a cup.

Grandma kept a record of their sales and told them they had earned a good amount of money.

She, however, told them they would not be able to buy toys that day, as they had not earned enough.

Besides, it was already late, and they would not be able to go into town.

They had dinner together and fell asleep as soon as they lay on the bed.

The next day, Pete suggested that they pick up some of the trash left by people on the beach.

They would then take what they picked up to be recycled, and they would get paid by the pound.

Their grandparents loved the idea, but Alice refused to pick up any trash. She was a princess after all!

With their gloves on and garbage bags in hand, they proceeded to pick bottles and items that could be recycled.

Alice tagged along and spent the day pointing out items that could be recycled. She was helpful in that way.

The task for the next day was collecting sea shells.

Grandma had told them that sea shells could be used for a lot of things, such as jewelry, window chimes and decorations. People in town usually paid well for them.

Grandpa instructed them not to go too close to the water, and they all went in search of the shells.

Pete led the way while Alice tagged along with her pigtails dancing behind her.

At the end of the day, they did not really collect as many shells as they thought they would.

They met other kids who also came to find shells, and they had so much fun playing around on the beach.

Alice and Pete wanted to get there early to collect more shells the next day.

They sold them all to the shop owner they met on the beach.

Grandma kept a record of their sales and told them they had earned more money.

Hula hooping was Alice's favorite thing in the world after her princess dolls.

She was quite good at twirling them on her waist and limbs at the same time.

Grandma suggested that she do hula hoop tricks to earn some money to add to their savings for the toys.

Pete made a sign for her and played the music to accompany Alice's show.

A number of people stopped by to watch, and they were impressed with the way Alice hula hooped.

They couldn't believe she was just four years old.

The next day, Grandpa told the kids that they would be picking up drift wood, and they would be able to sell it.

"But it's just wood, Grandpa. Nobody pays for wood," said Pete.

Grandpa smiled and told them that driftwood could be used to make decorations, signs and even art work.

They went eagerly to the beach and picked up quite a bit of driftwood.

The kids were very tired from all the walking around, so Grandpa helped them carry the wood.

They decided that they would take some driftwood home and have their parents help them sell it in the city.

Grandma told the kids that they could also pick up sea glass on the beach.

Sea glass is broken pieces of glass that resembles smooth stones or marbles, and they can be used in craft projects, art work and beach inspired designs.

Alice and Pete did not know what to look for, so Grandma went with them, and they picked very beautiful pieces.

They sold the glass to a collector, who had a stand on the beach, and went home happily.

Alice decided to keep a few pieces of sea glass for her mom and herself.

The next morning, Grandma informed the kids that they would not have to work anymore.

They had earned enough to buy toys for themselves, and Grandpa would take them into town to get the toys.

The kids spent the day indoors , telling stories, and recounting their experiences on the beach.

Grandma made a special cake with fresh strawberries, and everybody had so much to eat.

Alice and Pete were truly very happy.

It was a few days before the end of their summer trip, and Grandpa drove the children into town to get their toys.

The toy store was huge and had a wide variety of different kinds of toys.

The kids wanted to get everything, but Grandpa told them to pick out one or two of their favorite toys each.

Alice settled for a princess doll that came with some tea cups, while Pete selected a race car set.

The drive back to the beach house was fun, as Grandpa told them stories of summers spent on the beach.

The kids spent the next couple of days playing with their toys and helping their grandparents around the house.

The children discovered that they actually had a lot of fun on the beach even without their toys.

In the course of doing the various jobs, they had forgotten all about their old toys and the desire to buy new toys.

They had made new friends and learned many new things, like the use of sea glass and drift wood.

The process of getting money for the toys was as much fun as playing with them.

Alice and Pete decided they wanted to have their summer vacation with their grandparents every year.

The children woke up to sounds of laughter coming from the kitchen.

They ran down and saw their parents sitting in chairs and talking with Grandma and Grandpa.

With wide smiles, they ran into the waiting arms of their parents.

They said their goodbyes and began the journey back home.

"How was your summer?" Dad asked. Alice and Pete beamed and chorused, "It was the best summer ever. We learned how to buy amazing new toys with our very own money, and we had so much fun!"

Remember to Always Dream Big.
-Anthony L. Surrette

www.ingramcontent.com/pod-product-compliance
Lightning Source LLC
Chambersburg PA
CBHW041229040426

42444CB00002B/100